CW00661561

Witnesses to the Risen Christ

Addresses of Pope Francis

*All booklets are published thanks to the
generous support of the members of the
Catholic Truth Society*

CATHOLIC TRUTH SOCIETY
PUBLISHERS TO THE HOLY SEE

Contents

ISBN 978 1 86082 879 9

The Cross and Resurrection

The foundation of our faith

In our previous Catechesis, we reflected on the event of
the Resurrection of Jesus, in which the women played a
special role. I would like to reflect on its saving capacity.
What does the Resurrection mean for our life? And why
is our faith in vain without it? Our faith is founded on
Christ's death and Resurrection, just as a house stands on
its foundations: if they give way, the whole house collapses.
Jesus gave himself on the cross, taking the burden of our
sins upon himself and descending into the abyss of death,
then in the Resurrection he triumphed over them, took
them away and opened before us the path to rebirth and
to a new life.

The new life of Baptism

St Peter summed this up at the beginning of his First
Letter, as we heard: "Blessed be the God and Father of
our Lord Jesus Christ! By his great mercy we have been
born anew to a living hope through the Resurrection of
Jesus Christ from the dead, and to an inheritance which
is imperishable, undefiled, and unfading" (*1 P* 1:3-4).
The Apostle tells us that with the Resurrection of Jesus
something absolutely new happens: we are set free from

the slavery of sin and become children of God; that is, we are born to new life. When is this accomplished for us? In the sacrament of Baptism. In ancient times, it was customarily received through immersion. The person who was to be baptised walked down into the great basin of the Baptistery, stepping out of his clothes, and the Bishop or Priest poured water on his head three times, baptising him in the name of the Father, of the Son, and of the Holy Spirit. Then the baptised person emerged from the basin and put on a new robe, the white one; in other words, by immersing himself in the death and Resurrection of Christ he was born to new life. He had become a son of God. In his Letter to the Romans St Paul wrote: "you have received the spirit of sonship. When we cry 'Abba! Father!' it is the Spirit himself bearing witness with our spirit that we are children of God" (*Rm* 8:15-16).

The Spirit

It is the Spirit himself whom we received in Baptism who teaches us, who spurs us to say to God: "Father" or, rather, "Abba!", which means "papa" or "dad". Our God is like this: he is a dad to us. The Holy Spirit creates within us this new condition as children of God. And this is the greatest gift we have received from the Paschal Mystery of Jesus. Moreover, God treats us as children, he understands us, he forgives us, he embraces us, he loves us even when we err. In the Old Testament, the Prophet

Isaiah was already affirming that even if a mother could forget her child, God never forgets us at any moment (cf. *Is* 49:15). And this is beautiful!

The dignity of God's children

Yet this filial relationship with God is not like a treasure that we keep in a corner of our life but must be increased. It must be nourished every day with listening to the word of God, with prayer, with participation in the sacraments, especially Reconciliation and the Eucharist, and with love. We can live as children! And this is our dignity - we have the dignity of children. We should behave as true children! This means that every day we must let Christ transform us and conform us to him; it means striving to live as Christians, endeavouring to follow him in spite of seeing our limitations and weaknesses. The temptation to set God aside in order to put ourselves at the centre is always at the door, and the experience of sin injures our Christian life, our being children of God. For this reason we must have the courage of faith not to allow ourselves to be guided by the mentality that tells us: "God is not necessary, he is not important for you", and so forth. It is exactly the opposite: only by behaving as children of God, without despairing at our shortcomings, at our sins, only by feeling loved by him will our life be new, enlivened by serenity and joy. God is our strength! God is our hope!

We possess a sound hope

We must be the first to have this steadfast hope and we must be a visible, clear and radiant sign of it for everyone. The risen Lord is the hope that never fails, that never disappoints (cf. *Rm* 5:5). Hope does not let us down - the hope of the Lord! How often in our life do hopes vanish, how often do the expectations we have in our heart come to nothing! Our hope as Christians is strong, safe and sound on this earth, where God has called us to walk, and it is open to eternity because it is founded on God who is always faithful. We must not forget: God is always faithful to us. Being raised with Christ through Baptism, with the gift of faith, an inheritance that is incorruptible, prompts us to seek God's things more often, to think of him more often and to pray to him more. Being Christian is not just obeying orders but means being in Christ, thinking like him, acting like him, loving like him; it means letting him take possession of our life and change it, transform it and free it from the darkness of evil and sin.

Letting our lives point to God

Let us point out the risen Christ to those who ask us to account for the hope that is in us (cf. *1 P* 3:15). Let us point him out with the proclamation of the word, but above all with our lives as people who have been raised. Let us show the joy of being children of God, the freedom that living in Christ gives us which is true freedom, the freedom that saves us from the slavery of evil, of sin and of death! Looking at the heavenly homeland, we shall receive new light and fresh strength, both in our commitment and in our daily efforts. This is a precious service that we must give to this world of ours which all too often no longer succeeds in raising its gaze on high, no longer succeeds in raising its gaze to God.

Witnesses to the Risen Christ

The Apostles, Christ's first witnesses

I would like to reflect briefly on the passage from
the Acts of the Apostles that is read in the Liturgy
of the Third Sunday of Easter. This text says that the
Apostles' first preaching in Jerusalem filled the city
with the news that Jesus was truly risen in accordance
with the Scriptures and was the Messiah foretold by
the Prophets. The chief priests and elders of the city
were endeavouring to crush the nascent community of
believers in Christ and had the Apostles thrown into jail,
ordering them to stop teaching in his name. But Peter
and the other Eleven answered: "We must obey God
rather than men. The God of our fathers raised Jesus...
exalted him at at his right hand as Leader and Saviour...
And we are witnesses to these things, and so is the Holy
Spirit whom God has given to those who obey him" (*Ac*
5:29-32). They therefore had the Apostles scourged and
once again ordered them to stop speaking in the name of
Jesus. And they went away, as Scripture says, "rejoicing
that they were counted worthy to suffer dishonour for
the name" of Jesus (*Ac* 5:41).

The true source of strength

I ask myself: where did the first disciples find the strength to bear this witness? And that is not all: what was the source of their joy and of their courage to preach despite the obstacles and violence? Let us not forget that the Apostles were simple people; they were neither scribes nor doctors of the Law, nor did they belong to the class of priests. With their limitations and with the authorities against them how did they manage to fill Jerusalem with their teaching (cf. *Ac* 5:28)? It is clear that only the presence with them of the risen Lord and the action of the Holy Spirit can explain this fact. The Lord who was with them and the Spirit who was impelling them to preach explain this extraordinary fact. Their faith was based on such a strong personal experience of the dead and risen Christ that they feared nothing and no one, and even saw persecution as a cause of honour that enabled them to follow in Jesus's footsteps and to be like him, witnessing with their life.

Behaving like Jesus

This history of the first Christian community tells us something very important which applies to the Church in all times and also to us. When a person truly knows Jesus Christ and believes in him, that person experiences his presence in life as well as the power of his Resurrection and cannot but communicate this experience. And if this person meets with misunderstanding or adversity, he behaves like Jesus in his Passion: he answers with love and with the power of the truth. In praying the Regina Cæli, let us ask for the help of Mary Most Holy so that the Church throughout the world may proclaim the Resurrection of the Lord with candour and courage and give credible witness to it with signs of brotherly love. Brotherly love is the closest testimony we can give that Jesus is alive with us, that Jesus is risen. Let us pray in a special way for Christians who are suffering persecution; in our day there are so many Christians who are suffering persecution - so, so many, in a great many countries: let us pray for them, with love, from our heart. May they feel the living and comforting presence of the risen Lord.

Seated at the Right Hand of the Father

Jesus ascends to heaven

In the Creed we say that Jesus "ascended into heaven and is seated at the right hand of the Father". Jesus's earthly life culminated with the Ascension, when he passed from this world to the Father and was raised to sit on his right. What does this event mean? How does it affect our life? What does contemplating Jesus seated at the right hand of the Father mean? Let us permit the Evangelist Luke to guide us in this. Let us start from the moment when Jesus decided to make his last pilgrimage to Jerusalem. St Luke notes: "When the days drew near for him to be received up, he set his face to go to Jerusalem" (*Lk* 9:51). While he was "going up" to the Holy City, where his own "exodus" from this life was to occur, Jesus already saw the destination, heaven, but he knew well that the way which would lead him to the glory of the Father passed through the cross, through obedience to the divine design of love for mankind. The *Catechism of the Catholic Church* states that: "The lifting up of Jesus on the cross signifies and announces his lifting up by his Ascension into heaven" (n. 662).

Being faithful to God's plan

We too should be clear in our Christian life that entering the glory of God demands daily fidelity to his will, even when it demands sacrifice and sometimes requires us to change our plans. The Ascension of Jesus actually happened on the Mount of Olives, close to the place where he had withdrawn to pray before the Passion in order to remain in deep union with the Father: once again we see that prayer gives us the grace to be faithful to God's plan. At the end of his Gospel, St Luke gives a very concise account of the event of the Ascension. Jesus led his disciples "out as far as Bethany, and lifting up his hands he blessed them. While he blessed them, he parted from them, and was carried up into heaven. And they worshipped him, and returned to Jerusalem with great joy, and were continually in the temple blessing God" (*Lk* 24:50-53).

Jesus is our advocate

I would like to note two elements in the account. First of all, during the Ascension Jesus made the priestly gesture of blessing, and the disciples certainly expressed their faith with prostration, they knelt with bowed heads. This is the first important point: Jesus is the one eternal High Priest who with his Passion passed through death and the tomb and ascended into heaven. He is with God the Father where he intercedes for ever in our favour (cf. *Heb* 9:24).

As St John says in his First Letter, he is our advocate: how beautiful it is to hear this! When someone is summoned by the judge or is involved in legal proceedings, the first thing he does is to seek a lawyer to defend him. We have one who always defends us, who defends us from the snares of the Devil, who defends us from ourselves and from our sins! We have this advocate; let us not be afraid to turn to him to ask forgiveness, to ask for a blessing, to ask for mercy! He always pardons us, he is our advocate: he always defends us! Don't forget this!

Christ has opened the path to God

The Ascension of Jesus into heaven acquaints us with this deeply consoling reality on our journey: in Christ, true God and true man, our humanity was taken to God. Christ opened the path to us. He is like a roped guide climbing a mountain who, on reaching the summit, pulls us up to him and leads us to God. If we entrust our life to him, if we let ourselves be guided by him, we are certain to be in safe hands, in the hands of our Saviour, of our advocate.

Jesus remains with them and us

The second element: St Luke says that having seen Jesus ascending into heaven, the Apostles returned to Jerusalem "with great joy". This seems to us a little odd. When we are separated from our relatives, from our friends, because of a definitive departure and especially death, there is

14

usually a natural sadness in us since we will no longer see their face, no longer hear their voice or enjoy their love, their presence. The Evangelist instead emphasises the profound joy of the Apostles. But how could this be? Precisely because with the gaze of faith they understand that although he has been removed from their sight, Jesus stays with them for ever. He does not abandon them and in the glory of the Father supports them, guides them and intercedes for them.

Contemplation leads to action

St Luke too recounts the event of the Ascension - at the beginning of the Acts of the Apostles - to emphasise that this event is like the link of the chain that connects Jesus's earthly life to the life of the Church. Here St Luke also speaks of the cloud that hid Jesus from the sight of the disciples who stood gazing at him ascending to God (cf. *Ac* 1:9-10). Then two men in white robes appeared and asked them not to stand there looking up to heaven but to nourish their lives and their witness with the certainty that Jesus will come again in the same way in which they saw him ascending into heaven (cf. *Ac* 1:10-11). This is the invitation to base our contemplation on Christ's lordship, to find in him the strength to spread the gospel and to witness to it in everyday life: contemplation and action, *ora et labora*, as St Benedict taught, are both necessary in our life as Christians.

The eternally present Christ

The Ascension does not point to Jesus's absence, but tells us that he is alive in our midst in a new way. He is no longer in a specific place in the world as he was before the Ascension. He is now in the lordship of God, present in every space and time, close to each one of us. In our life we are never alone: we have this advocate who awaits us, who defends us. We are never alone: the crucified and risen Lord guides us. We have with us a multitude of brothers and sisters who, in silence and concealment, in their family life and at work, in their problems and hardships, in their joys and hopes, live faith daily and together with us bring the world the lordship of God's love, in the risen Jesus Christ, ascended into heaven, our own advocate who pleads for us.

The Good Shepherd

The Good Shepherd: the nucleus of the Gospel

The Fourth Sunday of the Season of Easter is characterised by the Gospel of the Good Shepherd - in chapter ten of St John - which is read every year. The passage records these words of Jesus: "My sheep hear my voice, and I know them, and they follow me; and I give them eternal life, and they shall never perish, and no one shall snatch them out of my hand. My Father, who has given them to me is greater than all, and no one is able to snatch them out of the Father's hand. I and the Father are one" (*Jn* 10:27-30). These four verses contain the whole of Jesus's message; it is the nucleus of his gospel: he calls us to share in his relationship with the Father, and this is eternal life.

The voice of Christ

Jesus wants to establish with his friends a relationship which mirrors his own relationship with the Father: a relationship of reciprocal belonging in full trust, in intimate communion. To express this profound understanding, this relationship of friendship, Jesus uses the image of the shepherd with his sheep: he calls them and they recognise his voice, they respond to his call and follow him. This parable is very beautiful! The mystery of his voice is evocative: only think that from our mother's womb we learn to recognise her voice and that of our father; it is from the tone of a voice that we perceive love or contempt, affection or coldness. Jesus's voice is unique! If we learn to distinguish it, he guides us on the path of life, a path that goes beyond even the abyss of death.

Listening for his call

However Jesus, at a certain point, said: "my Father, who has given them to me..." (*Jn* 10:29), referring to his sheep. This is very important, it is a profound mystery far from easy to understand. If I feel drawn to Jesus, if his voice warms my heart, it is thanks to God the Father who has sown within me the desire for love, for truth, for life, for beauty...and Jesus is all this in fullness! This helps us understand the mystery of vocation and especially of the call to a special consecration. Sometimes Jesus calls us, he invites us to follow him, but perhaps we do not realise that it is he who is calling, like what happened to the young Samuel. There are many young people today, here in the Square. There are large numbers of you aren't there? It's clear....look! Here in the square today there are so many of you! I would like to ask you: have you sometimes heard the Lord's voice, in a desire, in a worry, did he invite you to follow him more closely? Have you heard him? Have you wanted to be apostles of Jesus? We must bet on youth for the great ideals. Do you think this? Do you agree? Ask Jesus what he wants of you and be brave! Be brave! Ask him this!

Vocation is built on and from prayer

Behind and before every vocation to the priesthood or to the consecrated life there is always the strong and intense prayer of someone: a grandmother, a grandfather, a mother, a father, a [community]...this is why Jesus said: "Pray therefore the Lord of the harvest", that is, God the Father, "to send out labourers into his harvest" (*Mt* 9:38). Vocations are born in prayer and from prayer; and only through prayer can they persevere and bear fruit. I am pleased to stress this today, which is the "World Day of Prayer for Vocations". Let us pray in particular for the new Priests of the Diocese of Rome whom I have had the joy to ordain this morning. And let us invoke the intercession of Mary. Today there were 10 young men who said "yes" to Jesus and they have been ordained priests this morning. This is beautiful!

Learning from Our Lady

Let us invoke the intercession of Mary who is the Woman of the "yes". Mary said "yes" throughout her life! She learned to recognise Jesus's voice from the time when she carried him in her womb. May Mary, our Mother, help us to know Jesus's voice better and better and to follow it, so as to walk on the path of life! Thank you so much for your greeting, but greet Jesus too. Shout "Jesus" very loudly. Let us all pray together to Our Lady.

Judge of the Living and the Dead

History begins and ends with God

In the Creed we profess that Jesus "will come again in glory to judge the living and the dead". Human history begins with the creation of man and woman in God's likeness and ends with the Last Judgement of Christ. These two poles of history are often forgotten; and, at times, faith in Christ's return and in the Last Judgement, are not so clear and firm in Christian hearts. In his public life Jesus frequently reflected on the reality of his Final Coming. I would like to reflect on three Gospel texts that help us to penetrate this mystery: those of the ten virgins, of the talents and of the Last Judgement. All three are part of Jesus's discourse on the end of time which can be found in the Gospel of St Matthew.

Let us remember first of all that in the Ascension the Son of God brought to the Father our humanity, which he had taken on, and that he wants to draw all to himself, to call the whole world to be welcomed in God's embrace so that at the end of history the whole of reality may be consigned to the Father. Yet there is this "immediate time" between the First and the Final Coming of Christ, and that is the very time in which we are living.

The ten virgins

The parable of the ten virgins fits into this context of "immediate" time (cf. *Mt* 25:1-13). They are ten maidens who are awaiting the arrival of the Bridegroom, but he is late and they fall asleep. At the sudden announcement that the Bridegroom is arriving they prepare to welcome him. But while five of them, who are wise, have oil to burn in their lamps, the others, who are foolish, are left with lamps that have gone out because they have no oil. While they go to get some oil the Bridegroom arrives and the foolish virgins find that the door to the hall of the marriage feast is shut. They knock on it again and again but it is now too late; the Bridegroom answers: I do not know you.

Keeping our lamps alight

The Bridegroom is the Lord and the time of waiting for his arrival is the time he gives to us, to all of us, before his Final Coming with mercy and patience; it is a time of watchfulness; a time in which we must keep alight the lamps of faith, hope and charity, a time in which to keep our heart open to goodness, beauty and truth. It is a time to live in accordance with God, because we do not know either the day or the hour of Christ's return. What he asks of us is to be ready for an encounter, for a beautiful encounter, the encounter with Jesus, which means being able to see the signs of his presence, keeping our faith alive with prayer, with the sacraments, and taking care not to fall asleep so as to not forget about God. The life of slumbering Christians is a sad life. Christians must be happy, with the joy of Jesus. Let us not fall asleep!

The parable of the talents

The second parable, the parable of the talents, makes us think about the relationship between how we use the gifts we have received from God and his return, when he will ask us what use we made of them (cf. *Mt* 25:14-30). We are well acquainted with the parable: before his departure the master gives a few talents to each of his servants to ensure that they will be put to good use during his absence. He gives five to the first servant, two to the second one and one to the third. In the period of their master's absence, the first two servants increase their talents - these are ancient coins - whereas the third servant prefers to bury his and to return it to his master as it was. On his return, the master judges what they have done: he praises the first two while he throws the third one out into the outer darkness because, through fear, he had hidden his talent, withdrawing into himself. A Christian who withdraws into himself, who hides everything that the Lord has given him, is a Christian who...he is not a Christian! He is a Christian who does not thank God for everything God has given him!

The time of action

This tells us that the expectation of the Lord's return is the time of action - we are in the time of action - the time in which we should bring God's gifts to fruition, not for ourselves but for him, for the Church, for others. The time to seek to increase goodness in the world always; and in particular, in this period of crisis, it is important not to turn in on ourselves, burying our own talent, our spiritual, intellectual, and material riches, everything that the Lord has given us, but, rather to open ourselves, to be supportive, to be attentive to others.

A message to young people

In the square I have seen that there are many young people here: it is true, isn't it? Are there many young people? Where are they? I ask you who are just setting out on your journey through life: have you thought about the talents that God has given you? Have you thought of how you can put them at the service of others? Do not bury your talents! Set your stakes on great ideals, the ideals that enlarge the heart, the ideals of service that make your talents fruitful. Life is not given to us to be jealously guarded for ourselves, but is given to us so that we may give it in turn. Dear young people, have a deep spirit! Do not be afraid to dream of great things!

The Last Judgement

Lastly, a word about the passage on the Last Judgement in which the Lord's Second Coming is described, when he will judge all human beings, the living and the dead (cf. *Mt* 25:31-46). The image used by the Evangelist is that of the shepherd who separates the sheep from the goats. On his right he places those who have acted in accordance with God's will, who went to the aid of their hungry, thirsty, foreign, naked, sick or imprisoned neighbour - I said "foreign": I am thinking of the multitude of foreigners who are here in the Diocese of Rome: what do we do for them? While on his left are those who did not help their neighbour. This tells us that God will judge us on our love, on how we have loved our brethren, especially the weakest and the neediest. Of course we must always clearly have in mind that we are justified, we are saved through grace, through an act of freely-given love by God who always goes before us; on our own we can do nothing. Faith is first of all a gift we have received.

Corresponding with the love of Jesus

But in order to bear fruit, God's grace always demands our openness to him, our free and tangible response. Christ comes to bring us the mercy of a God who saves. We are asked to trust in him, to correspond to the gift of his love with a good life, made up of actions motivated by faith and love. May looking at the Last Judgement never frighten us: rather, may it impel us to live the present better. God offers us this time with mercy and patience so that we may learn every day to recognise him in the poor and in the lowly. Let us strive for goodness and be watchful in prayer and in love. May the Lord, at the end of our life and at the end of history, be able to recognise us as good and faithful servants.

Entrusting Ourselves to Our Lady

Accepting Jesus as Mary did

I would like to entrust to Our Lady the newly confirmed and all of you. The Virgin Mary teaches us what it means to live in the Holy Spirit and what it means to accept the news of God in our life. She conceived Jesus by the work of the Holy Spirit, and every Christian, each one of us, is called to accept the Word of God, to accept Jesus inside of us and then to bring him to everyone. Mary invoked the Holy Spirit with the Apostles in the Upper Room: we too, every time that we come together in prayer, are sustained by the spiritual presence of the Mother of Jesus, in order to receive the gift of the Spirit and to have the strength to bear witness to the Jesus Risen. I say this in a special way to you who have newly received Confirmation: may Mary help you to be attentive to what the Lord asks of you, and to live and walk forever with the Holy Spirit!

The Father and Mother of Jesus Christ

On the Feast of St Joseph the Worker

On 1st May we celebrate St Joseph the Worker and begin the month traditionally dedicated to Our Lady. I want to focus on these two figures, so important in the life of Jesus, the Church and in our lives, with two brief thoughts: the first on work, the second on the contemplation of Jesus.

Jesus's identity as St Joseph's son

In the Gospel of St Matthew, in one of the moments when Jesus returns to his town, to Nazareth, and speaks in the synagogue, the amazement of his fellow townspeople at his wisdom is emphasised. They asked themselves the question: "Is not this the carpenter's son?" (*Mk* 13:55). Jesus comes into our history, he comes among us by being born of Mary by the power of God, but with the presence of St Joseph, the legal father who cares for him and also teaches him his trade. Jesus is born and lives in a family, in the Holy Family, learning the carpenter's craft from St Joseph in his workshop in Nazareth, sharing with him the commitment, effort, satisfaction and also the difficulties of every day.

Work anoints us with divine dignity

This reminds us of the dignity and importance of work. The Book of Genesis tells us that God created man and woman entrusting them with the task of filling the earth and subduing it, which does not mean exploiting it but nurturing and protecting it, caring for it through their work (cf. *Gn* 1:28; 2:15). Work is part of God's loving plan, we are called to cultivate and care for all the goods of creation and in this way share in the work of creation! Work is fundamental to the dignity of a person. Work, to use a metaphor, "anoints" us with dignity, fills us with dignity, makes us similar to God, who has worked and still works, who always acts (cf. *Jn* 5:17); it gives one the ability to maintain oneself, one's family, to contribute to the growth of one's own nation. And here I think of the difficulties which, in various countries, afflict the world of work and business today; I am thinking of how many, and not only young people, are unemployed, often due to a purely economic conception of society, which seeks profit selfishly, beyond the parameters of social justice.

Acting like St Joseph

I wish to extend an invitation to solidarity to everyone, and I would like to encourage those in public office to make every effort to give new impetus to employment. This means caring for the dignity of the person, but above all I would say: do not lose hope. St Joseph also experienced moments of difficulty, but he never lost faith and was able to overcome them in the certainty that God never abandons us. And then I would like to speak especially to young people: be committed to your daily duties, your studies, your work, to relationships of friendship, to helping others; your future also depends on how you live these precious years of your life. Do not be afraid of commitment, of sacrifice and do not view the future with fear. Keep your hope alive: there is always a light on the horizon.

We must combat slavery

I would like to add a word about another particular work situation that concerns me: I am referring to what we could define as "slave labour", work that enslaves. How many people worldwide are victims of this type of slavery, when the person is at the service of his or her work, while work should offer a service to people so they may have dignity. I ask my brothers and sisters in the faith and all men and women of good will for a decisive choice to combat the trafficking in persons, in which "slave labour" exists.

Jesus, the centre of our daily life

With reference to the second thought: in the silence of the daily routine, St Joseph, together with Mary, share a single common centre of attention: Jesus. They accompany and nurture the growth of the Son of God made man for us with commitment and tenderness, reflecting on everything that happened. In the Gospels, St Luke twice emphasises the attitude of Mary, which is also that of St Joseph: she "kept all these things, pondering them in her heart" (*Lk* 2:19,51). To listen to the Lord we must learn to contemplate, feel his constant presence in our lives and we must stop and converse with him, give him space in prayer. Each of us, even you boys and girls, young people, so many of you here this morning, should ask yourselves: "how much space do I give to the Lord? Do I stop to talk with him?" Ever since we were children our parents have taught us to start and end the day with a prayer, to teach us to feel that the friendship and the love of God accompanies us. Let us remember the Lord more in our daily life!

Strengthening our family through the Rosary

In this month of May, I would like to recall the importance and beauty of the prayer of the Holy Rosary. Reciting the Hail Mary, we are led to contemplate the mysteries of Jesus, that is, to reflect on the key moments of his life, so that, as with Mary and St Joseph, he is the centre of our thoughts, of our attention and our actions. It would be nice if, especially in this month of May, we could pray the Holy Rosary together in the family, with friends, in the parish, or some prayer to Jesus and the Virgin Mary! Praying together is a precious moment that further strengthens family life and friendship! Let us learn to pray more in the family and as a family! Let us ask St Joseph and the Virgin Mary to teach us to be faithful to our daily tasks, to live our faith in the actions of everyday life and to give more space to the Lord in our lives, to pause to contemplate his face.

The Motherly Presence of Mary

Devotion to Our Lady

At this moment of profound communion with Christ, we also feel among us the living presence of the Virgin Mary. It is a motherly presence, a familial presence, especially for you who are part of the confraternity. Love for Our Lady is one of the characteristics of popular devotion that must be respected and well directed. For this reason, I invite you to meditate on the last chapter of the Constitution of the Second Vatican Council on the Church, *Lumen Gentium*, which speaks of Mary in the mystery of Christ and of the Church. There it says that Mary "advanced in her pilgrimage of faith" (n. 58). In the Year of Faith I leave you this icon of Mary the pilgrim, who follows her Son Jesus and precedes us all in the journey of faith.

The Holy Spirit

The season of the Holy Spirit

The Easter Season that we are living joyfully, guided by
the Church's liturgy, is *par excellence* the season of the
Holy Spirit given "without measure" (cf. *Jn* 3:34) by Jesus
crucified and risen. This time of grace closes with the Feast
of Pentecost, in which the Church relives the outpouring of
the Spirit upon Mary and the Apostles gathered in prayer
in the Upper Room. But who is the Holy Spirit? In the
Creed we profess with faith: "I believe in the Holy Spirit,
the Lord and Giver of life". The first truth to which we
adhere in the Creed is that the Holy Spirit is *Kýrios*, Lord.
This signifies that he is truly God just as the Father and the
Son; the object, on our part, of the same act of adoration
and glorification that we address to the Father and to the
Son. Indeed, the Holy Spirit is the Third Person of the
Most Holy Trinity; he is the great gift of the risen Christ
who opens our mind and our heart to faith in Jesus as the
Son sent by the Father and who leads us to friendship, to
communion with God.

The source of God's life in us

However, I would like to focus especially on the fact that
the Holy Spirit is the inexhaustible source of God's life in

us. Man in every time and place desires a full and beautiful life, just and good, a life that is not threatened by death, but can still mature and grow to fullness. Man is like a traveller who, crossing the deserts of life, thirsts for the living water: gushing and fresh, capable of quenching his deep desire for light, love, beauty and peace. We all feel this desire! And Jesus gives us this living water: he is the Holy Spirit, who proceeds from the Father and whom Jesus pours out into our hearts. "I came that they may have life, and have it abundantly", Jesus tells us (*Jn* 10:10).

The 'living water'

Jesus promised the Samaritan woman that he will give a superabundance of "living water" forever to all those who recognise him as the Son sent by the Father to save us (cf. *Jn* 4:5-26; 3:17). Jesus came to give us this "living water", who is the Holy Spirit, that our life might be guided by God, might be moved by God, nourished by God. When we say that a Christian is a spiritual being we mean just this: the Christian is a person who thinks and acts in accordance with God, in accordance with the Holy Spirit. But I ask myself: do we think in accordance with God? Do we act in accordance with God? Or do we let ourselves be guided by the many other things that certainly do not come from God? Each one of us needs to respond to this in the depths of his or her own heart.

Participating in the life of God

At this point we may ask ourselves: why can this water quench our thirst deep down? We know that water is essential to life; without water we die; it quenches, washes, makes the earth fertile. In the Letter to the Romans we find these words: "God's love has been poured into our hearts through the Holy Spirit who has been given to us" (*Rm* 5:5). The "living water", the Holy Spirit, the Gift of the Risen One who dwells in us, purifies us, illuminates us, renews us, transforms us because he makes us participants in the very life of God that is Love. That is why the Apostle Paul says that the Christian's life is moved by the Holy Spirit and by his fruits, which are "love, joy, peace, patience, kindness, goodness, faithfulness, gentleness, self-control" (*Ga* 5:22-23). *The Holy Spirit introduces us to divine life as "children in the Only-Begotten Son"*.

Divine sonship

In another passage from the Letter to the Romans, that we have recalled several times, St Paul sums it up with these words: "For all who are led by the Spirit of God are sons of God. For you...have received the spirit of sonship. When we cry, 'Abba! Father!' it is the Spirit himself bearing witness with our spirit that we are children of God, and if children, then heirs, heirs of God and fellow heirs with Christ, provided we suffer with him in order that we may also be glorified with him" (*Rm* 8:14-17).

This is the precious gift that the Holy Spirit brings to our hearts: the very life of God, the life of true children, a relationship of confidence, freedom and trust in the love and mercy of God. It also gives us a new perception of others, close and far, seen always as brothers and sisters in Jesus to be respected and loved.

Listening to the Holy Spirit

The Holy Spirit teaches us to see with the eyes of Christ, to live life as Christ lived, to understand life as Christ understood it. That is why the living water, who is the Holy Spirit, quenches our life, why he tells us that we are loved by God as children, that we can love God as his children and that by his grace we can live as children of God, like Jesus. And we, do we listen to the Holy Spirit? What does the Holy Spirit tell us? He says: God loves you. He tells us this. God loves you, God likes you. Do we truly love God and others, as Jesus does? Let us allow ourselves to be guided by the Holy Spirit, let us allow him to speak to our heart and say this to us: God is love, God is waiting for us, God is Father, he loves us as a true father loves, he loves us truly and only the Holy Spirit can tell us this in our hearts. Let us hear the Holy Spirit, let us listen to the Holy Spirit and may we move forward on this path of love, mercy and forgiveness.

The Presence of new Saints in the Church

Invoking the Saints' powerful intercession

May the martyrs of Otranto help the beloved Italian people to look with hope to the future, trusting in the closeness of God who never abandons us, even in difficult moments.

Through the intercession of Mother Laura Montoya may the Lord grant the Church a new missionary and evangelising impetus and, inspired by this new saint's example of harmony and reconciliation may the beloved sons and daughters of Colombia continue to work for peace and for the just development of their homeland. Let us place in the hands of St Guadalupe García Zavala all the poor, the sick and those who care for them. Let us also commend to her intercession the noble Mexican nation so that all violence and insecurity may be eradicated and that it may continue to advance on the path of solidarity and brotherly co-existence.

Respect for the sick and the unborn

I am now glad to recall the beatification of the priest Luigi Novarese, founder of the International Confederation of the Volunteers of Suffering Centres and of the Silent Workers of the Cross. I join in the thanksgiving for this exemplary priest, who was able to renew the pastoral care of the sick by giving them an active role in the Church.

I greet the participants in the March for Life which took place this morning in Rome. I ask everyone to continue to pay special attention to this most important issue of respect for human life from the moment of conception. In this regard I would also like to remember the collection of signatures being made today in Italian parishes in support of the European project "One of Us". The initiative aims to guarantee embryos legal protection, safeguarding every human being from the very first moment of his or her existence. *Evangelium Vitae* Day is a special event for those who have at heart the defence of the sacred nature of human life.

The Church, the Truth and the Holy Spirit

The Holy Spirit guides us to the Truth

I would like to reflect on the Holy Spirit's action in guiding the Church and each one of us to the Truth. Jesus himself told his disciples: "[the Holy Spirit] will guide you into all the truth" (*Jn* 16:13), since he himself is "the Spirit of Truth" (cf. *Jn* 14:17; 15:26; 16:13).

We are living in an age in which people are rather sceptical of truth. Benedict XVI has frequently spoken of relativism, that is, of the tendency to consider nothing definitive and to think that truth comes from consensus or from something we like. The question arises: does "the" truth really exist? What is "the" truth? Can we know it? Can we find it? Here springs to my mind the question of Pontius Pilate, the Roman Procurator, when Jesus reveals to him the deep meaning of his mission: "What is truth?" (*Jn* 18:37,38). Pilate cannot understand that "the" Truth is standing in front of him, he cannot see in Jesus the face of the truth that is the face of God. And yet Jesus is exactly this: the Truth that, in the fullness of time, "became flesh" (cf. *Jn* 1:1,14), and came to dwell among us so that we might know it. The truth is not grasped as a thing, the truth is encountered. It is not a possession, it is an encounter with a Person.

Recognising the Truth

But who can enable us to recognise that Jesus is "the" Word of Truth, the Only-Begotten Son of God the Father? St Paul teaches that "no one can say 'Jesus is Lord' except by the Holy Spirit" (*1 Co* 12:3). It is the Holy Spirit himself, the gift of the risen Christ, who makes us recognise the Truth. Jesus describes him as the "Paraclete", namely, "the one who comes to our aid", who is beside us to sustain us on this journey of knowledge; and at the Last Supper Jesus assures the disciples that the Holy Spirit will teach them all things and remind them of all he has said to them (cf. *Jn* 14:26).

The Holy Spirit transforms our heart

So how does the Holy Spirit act in our life and in the life of the Church in order to guide us to the truth? First of all he recalls and impresses in the heart of believers the words Jesus spoke and, through these very words, the law of God - as the Prophets of the Old Testament had foretold - is engraved in our heart and becomes within us a criterion for evaluation in decisions and for guidance in our daily actions; it becomes a principle to live by. Ezekiel's great prophesy is brought about: "You shall be clean from all your uncleannesses, and from all your idols I will cleanse you. A new heart I will give you, and a new spirit I will put within you.... And I will put my spirit within you, and cause you to walk in my statutes and be careful to observe my ordinances" (*Ezk* 36:25-27). Indeed, it is in our inmost depths that our actions come into being: it is the heart itself that must be converted to God and the Holy Spirit transforms it when we open ourselves to him.

Our guide "into" the fullness of the Truth

Then, as Jesus promised, the Holy Spirit guides us "into all the truth" (*Jn* 16:13); not only does he guide us to the encounter with Jesus, the fullness of the Truth, but he also guides us "into" the Truth, that is, he makes us enter into an ever deeper communion with Jesus, giving us knowledge of all the things of God. And we cannot achieve this by our own efforts. Unless God enlightens us from within, our Christian existence will be superficial. The Church's Tradition asserts that the Spirit of Truth acts in our heart, inspiring that "sense of the Faith" (*sensus fidei*) through which, as the Second Vatican Council states, the People of God, under the guidance of the Magisterium, adheres unfailingly to the Faith transmitted, penetrates it more deeply with the right judgement, and applies it more fully in life (cf. Dogmatic Constitution *Lumen Gentium*, n. 12). Let us try asking ourselves: am I open to the action of the Holy Spirit? Do I pray him to give me illumination, to make me more sensitive to God's things?

Praying to the Holy Spirit

This is a prayer we must pray every day: "Holy Spirit, make my heart open to the word of God, make my heart open to goodness, make my heart open to the beauty of God every day". I would like to ask everyone a question: how many of you pray every day to the Holy Spirit? There will not be many but we must fulfil Jesus's wish and pray every day to the Holy Spirit that he opens our heart to Jesus. Let us think of Mary who "kept all these things, pondering them in her heart" (*Lk* 2:19,51). Acceptance of the words and truth of faith so that they may become life is brought about and increases under the action of the Holy Spirit. In this regard we must learn from Mary, we must re-live her "yes", her unreserved readiness to receive the Son of God in her life, which was transformed from that moment. Through the Holy Spirit, the Father and the Son take up their abode with us: we live in God and are [of God]. Yet is our life truly inspired by God? How many things do I put before God?

We cannot be "part-time" Christians

We need to let ourselves be bathed in the light of the Holy Spirit so that he may lead us into the Truth of God, who is the one Lord of our life. In this Year of Faith let us ask ourselves whether we really have taken some steps to know Christ and the truth of faith better by reading and meditating on Sacred Scripture, by studying the *Catechism* and by receiving the sacraments regularly. However, let us ask ourselves at the same time what steps we are taking to ensure that faith governs the whole of our existence. We are not Christian "part-time", only at certain moments, in certain circumstances, in certain decisions; no one can be Christian in this way, we are Christian all the time! Totally! May Christ's truth, which the Holy Spirit teaches us and gives to us, always and totally affect our daily life. Let us call on him more often so that he may guide us on the path of disciples of Christ. Let us call on him every day. I am making this suggestion to you: let us invoke the Holy Spirit every day, in this way the Holy Spirit will bring us close to Jesus Christ.

Pentecost

The Unity of the Church in the Upper Room

This celebration of faith is drawing to a close. It began with the Vigil and culminated with the Eucharist. It was a renewed Pentecost that transformed St Peter's Square into an Upper Room beneath the open sky. We have relived the experience of the nascent Church, harmonised in prayer with Mary, the Mother of Jesus (cf. *Ac* 1:14). In the variety of charisms we too have experienced the beauty of unity, of being one. Moreover this is an action of the Holy Spirit who creates unity in the Church ever anew. I would like to thank all the movements, associations, communities and ecclesial groups. You are a gift and a treasure in the Church! This is what you are! I thank in particular all of you who have come from Rome and from so many parts of the world. Always convey the power of the Gospel! Do not be afraid! Always feel joy and enthusiasm for communion in the Church! May the risen Lord be with you constantly and may Our Lady protect you!

Sources

This book draws together the Wednesday Audience Catecheses and Regina Cæli addresses of Pope Francis, which took place in St Peter's Square between 10th April 2013 and 19th May 2013:

The Cross and Resurrection: General Audience, 10 April 2013.

Witnesses to the Risen Christ: Regina Cæli on the Third Sunday of Easter, 14th April 2013.

Seated at the Right Hand of the Father: General Audience, 17th April 2013.

The Good Shepherd: Regina Cæli on the Fourth Sunday of Easter, 21st April 2013.

Judge of the Living and the Dead: General Audience, 24th April 2013.

Entrusting Ourselves to Our Lady: Regina Cæli on the Fifth Sunday of Easter, 28th April 2013.

The Father and Mother of Jesus Christ: General Audience, 1st May 2013.

The Motherly Presence of Mary: Regina Cæli on the Sixth Sunday of Easter, 5th May 2013.

The Holy Spirit: General Audience, 8th May 2013.

The Presence of new Saints in the Church: Regina Cæli on the Seventh Sunday of Easter, 12th May 2013.

The Church, the Truth and the Holy Spirit: General Audience, 15th May 2013.

Pentecost: Regina Cæli on the Solemnity of Pentecost, 19th May 2013.

How to spread the Gospel

Compiled by Fr Donncha Ó hAodha

We are all called to spread our faith. In this virtual dialogue, an imaginary Catholic considers the challenges raised by evangelisation. The questions that he asks raise issues we might all encounter whilst trying to spread the Gospel successfully. The responses offered are taken from different instances of the preaching of Pope Emeritus Benedict XVI. This teaching is joyful and filled with hope, and makes evangelisation a service rather than a hardship, affirming everyone in their mission to be a fruitful apostle.

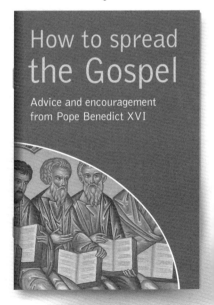

How to spread the Gospel

Advice and encouragement from Pope Benedict XVI

Do847   ISBN 978 1 86082 751 8

Pope Francis

Dushan Croos SJ

In the brief time the newly elected Pope Francis spent on the balcony of St Peter's to greet his new diocese in Rome, many the world over were left asking who this man was who gave such a great impression of humility and approachability. This newly written biography tells the story of Jorge Mario Bergoglio's journey from modest beginnings in Buenos Aires, through his studies in chemistry to formation in the Society of Jesus, then as Archbishop in Buenos Aires and finally to the See of Peter.

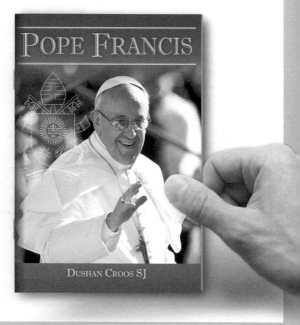

B752   ISBN 978 1 86082 870 6